HUMANOPHONE

For Faith –
with admiration for your work,
and with love –
Janet
7.3.2002
St. Paul, MN

HUMANOPHONE

Janet Holmes

Janet Holmes

University of Notre Dame Press
Notre Dame, Indiana

Manufactured in the United States of America

Library of Congress Cataloging-in-Publication Data
Holmes, Janet (Janet A.)
Humanophone / Janet Holmes.
p.   cm.
Includes bibliographical references (p.   ).
ISBN 0-268-03054-5 (cloth : alk. paper)
ISBN 0-268-03055-3 (pbk. : alk. paper)
1. Music—Poetry. I. Title.
PS3558.O35935   H8   2001
811'.54—dc21
                                        2001002294

In memory of

Eric Stokes (1930–99)

composer, teacher, enthusiast, friend

Contents

Acknowledgments

Grateful acknowledgment is made to the following publications, in which some of these poems appeared, sometimes in different forms.

American Poetry Review ("Reading Dante")
Beloit Poetry Journal ("Partch Stations")
Boulevard ("Mediterranean Cooking for Two")
Cider Press Review ("Lake Superior, Summer")
Fish Stories ("Fantasie Metropolitan")
Idaho Review ("Month After Month")
Laurel Review ("Kumquats," "Trappings")
Nimrod ("Celebration on the Planet Mars," "Humanophone," "Whistle")
Notre Dame Review ("Theremin," "Three Performances," "Wrong House")
Poetry International ("Lauds")
Prairie Schooner ("Depressive Episode")
Quarterly West ("Birding," "Glissando")
Tar River Poetry ("Prodigy")

"Celebration on the Planet Mars," "Humanophone," and "Whistle" were awarded first place in the 1997 Pablo Neruda Prize awards, one of the Ruth Hardman Awards from *Nimrod* magazine.

"Partch Stations" was awarded the 1999 Chad Walsh Prize from *Beloit Poetry Journal*.

"Trappings" appears also in *The Gazelle Poets Anthology: Volume One, Number One*, published by The Gazelle Poets through the City of Chicago Department of Cultural Affairs and the Illinois Arts Council, 1999.

"Depressive Episode" appears also in *Outsiders* (ed. Laure-Anne Bosselaar), Milkweed Editions, 1999.

"Depressive Episode," "Fantasie Metropolitan," and "Whistle" appear also in *The Extraordinary Tide* (ed. Suzanne Aizenberg and Erin Belieu), Columbia University Press, 2001.

Thanks to the Minnesota State Arts Board, the Jerome Foundation, the McKnight Foundation, The Loft, the editors of *Beloit Poetry Journal*, Alison Walsh Sackett, the editors of *Nimrod* magazine, and Ruth Hardman, as much for their generosity as for the encouragement and sustenance their awards provided. Likewise, my deep gratitude to W. S. Merwin. These poems would not have been possible without the fellowship, support, and generous criticism of other poets, chief among them Terri Ford, Alvin Greenberg, Kath Jesme, Jeffrey Levine, John Matthias, G. E. Patterson, Francine Sterle, and Stephanie Strickland. My students in the M.F.A. program at Boise State University are perhaps the best teachers of all.

HUMANOPHONE

Whistle

1.

says Come here, says
Hi, says Go Team,
one note or two:
you call the dog,
he comes wagging;
you call someone
(maybe a child)
and the child knows
to come when you
whistle for her—

At the ballpark,
at the concert,
use your fingers
and screech, you, on
the winning side,
high-pitched: better
than air horns. You
know what's good, and
she's a *good* child,
covering her
ears.

      Greet. Command.
Urge—

      Here I am!
Across the square!
Get over here!
You! Now!
      Yes, you—

2.

Hold the grassblade here,
between your thumbs. Now

cup your hands.

                    Put your
lips to the small spout
of your knuckles: make
a flute of the grass.

When you breathe, the blade
trembles: you blow, it
sings for you.

            Easy.

3.

And the puckery kind,
the melodic, carrying
its own tune: that's when you're
a musical instrument—
and you know what that's like,

being an instrument,
don't you? Everybody does
this one. You force the shape
of your mouth small, small, and make
the sounds, the tremolos,

the Whistle While You Work,
the Bridge Over the River
Kwai. It can be pretty.
It can keep you company
later, when you're alone.

4.

Those two notes: every parrot,
every construction worker
knows them and can perform. You
are meant to remember: *you
are on display.* It's supposed
to make you feel good, that they
have labored to remind you.

5.

This is least satisfactory,
but the only one I can do.
(And I can't wink with my left eye,
only with this one.)
                    Part your teeth,
a little. Then send out your breath:
sounds like wind with a bit of pitch
attached. Can't hear it far away.
Useless for calling, for making
most tunes. It's only a little
puff
        of the breath you weren't holding—

Glissando

Only once I remember my mother's father
taking from its plush-lined case
the trombone he jazzed decades before me,

taking it up to blow down a goofy slide,
the thrilling chute of its plummet
—defghijklmn-ohhhhh—

and a few high tootles
to get his lip back into it, his face
reddened, and mine—

oh, rapt! I suspect—and *encore*
in the eyes—before someone scooted in
to shush or interrupt us

and he only played one phrase more,
this time upwards
—zyxwvutsrqp-ohhhhh—

continuous, cartoony, a backwards pratfall
in brass. Of course I laughed.
He unscrewed the mouthpiece. And what,

I wonder now, could I have managed, what
conjuring would it have taken
to pull a whole song out of him

note by low note, or out
of that house?

Trappings

There's an Impala filled with mannequins
parked at the ice cream shop,
mannequins dressed as brides, all veiled.

I'm standing there with a drippy cone, looking.
The driver comes out. "How do you like
my ladies?" he asks, swinging into his seat,
revving, screeching, gone.

                        I hadn't been quite sure
they weren't really *real* women,
perhaps being dropped off for their weddings
at different churches by a nuptial
livery service—
               could have sworn
one turned her head to gaze at me—

or maybe being *picked up* from church,
having had second thoughts at the altar.

Runaway brides craving something
creamy, sweet, and cold.

    The girl doesn't know there *is* such a thing
as a veil salesman, probably thinks
dresses like this grow in dreams.
Like that painter, you start
with the naked body, then dress it
layer by layer—

                    chiffon, gossamer,
        then taffeta, taffeta, taffeta—

        lovingly, but the love of course
        never shows:
        anything diaphanous can hide it.

        The trick is to choose a fabric so sheer
        a man can't resist running it through his hands
        before he seizes what it seemed to cover.

Later, I thought, it wasn't a getaway car.
I figured he had a collection:
life-sized dolls!
Perhaps he takes them driving now and then.
At home, all five sit with him
around a formal table playing Reception:
who, this time, gets to sit with the groom? And at night,
does he lay them down in rows
in a king-sized bed, or tuck them in,
each in her own dark box, where she stays
'til morning?

        Song of the Veil Salesman

        This little bride wore organza,
        this little missy wore gauze,
        this little wife-to-be wore pointelle lace,
        this little lady wore tulle;
        and this little sweetie sang taffeta! taffeta! taffeta! taffeta!

        all the way home!

Saintmaker

It's straw the cross sparkles with, looking gold.
He sticks it there with a two-edged Gillette blade.

Tin can cut to a crown for the Queen of Heaven, paper clip unbent
into rabbit ears for the saint's

TV set, Santa Clara, patroness of visions.
His neighbor wants two of San Judas, one for each of her sons.

Three in the morning, he has wheeled himself out
into the air, having a smoke, carrying the half-finished crucifix flat

in his lap: it is Lent. Each year he gives God a crucifix:
his penance.

Olivar says: when the *santo* does not carry
your prayer,

turn him to the wall to teach him a lesson. That's
what the old people do. That's

their relationship. Insomniac, if I look
across to him, I meet the coal of his Camel head-on: black

cave of the breezeway, the *santero* its red center.

Prodigy

In the rest of his life he wants what children want:
his mother's attention, sweets, his own way. But he can't

have everything. The piano gives in so easily,
offering up the puzzles of its black and white keys

to his mindless solving touch, and he
is *genius, genius,* to his teacher, mother, everybody . . .

It's almost a trick, what he can do without
loving it,

what he hears missing in a virtuoso's performance
and brings to his own, instantly: nuance

and breath and preternatural knowledge: wise
execution, unfathomable. Easy to praise

his precision—but *spirit,* in a little boy,
emotional maturity,

where did that come from? He attacks
his own limits during practice:

facility, deception. Wants
what others seem to get from him—the experience

of transport, of joy—
wants to *play*—

Wrong House

Candle in this corner, *good*. Fame, wealth.
There, it will ruin your marriage.
La, la: here comes a woman setting the talismans right.
Don't look.
And the bed faces an inauspicious direction . . .

Come with her into the garden, we say "back yard."
Mostly because of no flowers—

Good Neighbor on the north we never see him.
Bad Neighbor's daughter screams on her trike
all the way to the south.
La: the view from the door is not blocked by the staircase:
All good.

Under the stairs, a cave for the child not home.
The perfect size for her, with a tiny entrance.
See, you're too big!

There should be a round mirror in your salon, says the woman:
Let me fix it.

(Our game was prying the heating grates open,
crawling inside: a secret room for kids,
for the littlest ones.
You got dirty . . .)

We can put up an altar there, it'll be lucky.
It's happiness. It's love—

and it turns out children are quite resilient.
A candle, a peacock's blue feather:
La, la.

Celebration on the Planet Mars

Music develops what I call a satellite, or orbital,
effect. It keeps going round and round in your mind . . .
                                                    —Raymond Scott

I. In His Mind's Ear

The six of them, his Quintette: Raymond Scott
surveys his sidemen from the piano as Ptolemy
plotted the moon and planets and sun
around his dominant Earth;

        and it's sphere music for sure he's set them spinning.

Where there's no sound
close to the one he needs, he directs the trumpeter
to dunk his bell in a bucket, playing the water,
the anodized pail, a muted echo of what's
in his mind's ear

because the time he's ahead of drags and drags.
Here's the missionary burbling in the cauldron,
warbling "Dinner Music
for a Pack of Hungry Cannibals."
Nothing you've heard before.

A seduction of sounds. He wants to lure them
down out of the galaxies, into the listening air.
He will lay for them mechanical traps, tempt them
into giving up their names: but for now
he calls the water to work for him simply,
as if it were breath.

II. "Celebration on the Planet Mars"

On the planet Mars they're dancing again,
swinging to jazzy sax in the red, discordant atmosphere,
and at the New York Aquarium
the penguins are swaying in their cage
as a writer for *down beat*—"The tenor sax solos
appeared to have the greatest effect on the birds"—
plays them "The Penguin" and solemnly
observes. The penguins spread their ineffectual wings,
spin uneven circles. They couldn't explain themselves
even if they could speak,
                          like the revelers on the red planet
who think of this music as "otherworldly,"
but of what other world? Sirenic, it compels them
forward, as one is compelled to do something foolish
or something new, toward
a kind of bravery.

III. Orbital Effect

Shirley Temple taps with Bill Robinson
in a screening room, in an endless
film loop; the cartoon rabbit
barrels along to "Powerhouse," outwitting the dumb hunter
another million times . . .

You can't stop humming.

Each time it's new:
endorphin tunes.

"I want to write music people would like
the first time they heard it," he said, knowing
that then people would never stop

hearing it.

IV. The Jazz Laboratory

He wants to lure them down out of the galaxies,
those elusive reverberations—had meant
to be training his ears to the ether all along,

high school radio wonk turned composer. He wants
an expansion of the lexicon of sound:
how else to set an accompaniment

to the lightspeed future? One needs
new notes, language soldered together
bit by bit in a jazz laboratory,

shot through with electric current
to see whether it breathes by itself. Karloff,
he names it, a machine that sizzles

convincingly as bacon, or wheezes like an asthmatic;
but to build his Clavivox he must use
some of its innards;

the result, a machine that sings
with a human voice, eery
as ectoplasm. In time,

it too gives up its fabricated life:
first to the Videola, then to synthesizers,
sequencers, a scanning radio, even

a serial doorbell;
today, only the Electronium
survives. The man

never applied for a single patent,
who had thirty-two feet of equipment
crowding his workshop,

the lights blinking Mardi Gras
in the artificial heat.
The Electronium cannot, he said, be used

to perform existing music.
It is designed for the instantaneous
composition-performance

of music heard only once,
then left to echo
in its solitary orbit . . .

V. "Dedicatory Piece to the Crew and Passengers of the First
Experimental Rocket Express to the Moon"

In the future, he said, the composer
will sit alone on the concert stage
and merely *think*
his idealized conception of his music

which will be channeled
directly into the minds of his hearers,

allowing for no distortion.

In this way would the seduction be complete:
sounds so compliant as to dance themselves
into the heads of an audience, without
the duenna of technology to mediate . . .

no saxophone, no keyboard. All body.
Human.

Come down, one says
to the symphony in the ether.

Be heard.

Reading Dante

e come vespa che ritragge l'ago,
a sé traendo la coda maligna,
trasse del fondo, e gissen vago vago.
                    —*Purgatorio* XXXII

That repeated word is the problem: either the dragon, whose tail has torn out part of the holy chariot's floor, is wiggling off as serpents are wont to do ("think of our word 'vagary'"),

which is what John seems to think,

or his pleasure is wickedly intensified (thus the doubled adjective), and he is pleased with himself beyond all reason: gloating: smug: he's taking part of the Church with him,

which is Charles's interpretation;

and of the commentaries, Ciardi agrees with John and Singleton with Charles, so that's no help. We can't decide.

It's a spring morning in Santa Fe. Forgive me, I have wandered through the window of the sunlit seminar room into the moist green yard where the corgi is sunning himself,

thinking that *vago* sounds, well, feminine to me,

and the word *smug* reminds me of Smaug, another dragon from literature. And as we go on with our class considering heresies alluded to, and whether Muhammad might be considered a Schismatic, if you lived in 1300,

no one expects me to say much. I'm not a morning person.

The birds are mad in the trees with their singing; the corgi doesn't care. He was out courting for three days, Charles says (who owns him), and he came back kind of beat up. Someone's in heat,

probably more dog than the corgi can handle. Somewhere, a bitch will whelp short-legged pups.

"*Vago*'s the third rhyme in a terza rima," I might point out. Though it *is* Italian, which English-speaking poets swear is an easier language to rhyme in,

I'll bet even Dante stretched for his third rhymes sometimes, and the result wasn't as sensible and mellifluous as he'd have liked. No,

I'm quiet at the table, the Italian in front of me, the English trot partly hidden beneath it. Lucky Dante gets to go to heaven. The terrifying angel has removed, with blows of his wings, the signs of Dante's sinful early life,

while the corgi and I will never get so far. We will pass each other forever on the winds of the first *cerchio,*

sighing. It's where we belong. Maybe over the eons he'll catch a glimpse of me: he'll wag, and I'll sigh back, *Good dog. It's this book,* I'll tell the earthly visitor,

that brought us together.

Fantasie Metropolitan

A ways off, someone is singing as he walks
down West End Avenue after the opera's done,
and the neighborhood of open windows looks

like balconies now hushed for him: a tux
here, and, radiant, a stylish sequined ballgown
a ways off shimmers . . . Singing as he walks,

he outdoes Luciano, Placido; he shocks
an eavesdropping producer ("Perfect tone!");
a neighborhood of open windows looks

down upon him, beaming (a young boy mocks
his carriage; but that's what you get from children).
A ways off, someone is listening as he walks

towards her, singing, unaware; she shakes
her hair: *What's that?* Attention caught, the one
discerning neighbor among the windows looks

up from her sofa: a warm evening, her book's
half finished. She'd like a glass of wine.
A ways off, someone is singing as he walks
her neighborhood. She opens the window. Looks.

Accident of Survival

The tiny baptismal dress wouldn't fit most dolls, let alone
an infant princess wiggling in a royal nurse's arms!
Handmade lace fragile as her eyelashes . . .

and queens wore clothing sewn—not for midgets, quite,
but for a perfectly proportioned smaller race.
The Antique Court Dress exhibit seems to argue

that royal creatures were all short and slight—or that,
as recently as a century ago, we were, each of us,
diminutive, scaled down . . .

                              and it sometimes seems,
in an antique apparel shop, that the petite
are responsible for the cream of the inventory,

all the beaded shifts sized four, or two . . .
How clumsy and big we are, leaving
these massive marks as we go, gouging the landscape

like Gulliver tracking sinkholes and clearcuts behind us!
It's comforting to imagine a delicate past.
Touring the Shoe Museum, you'd think this crowd

of miniature slippers, these sandals, clogs, and boots
were proof of our elfin and exotic ancestry.
Instead: they're accidents, the hand-me-downs

no Cinderella fit, no sister was small-boned enough
to borrow. Behold the silk-fringed dress,
custom-made for a slender single girl

who, following that season of bright parties (she the naughty,
she the daring one), folded it away to keep it safe.
How many years after that did she draw it out, thinking

this daughter, or that one, or a niece?
                                        —Each of them
born with her father's shoulders, and grown taller,

and anyway not interested in the bygone style
that once delighted the frail, shrunken-up old woman
who brought it *here* . . .

Three Performances

The lie is that he must be transparent
to let something through,

when what he must be is impenetrable
and still let it through.

Let x equal Bach, for example,
not what Bach is *like*.

What look to be obstacles
facilitate: the overcoat, the gloves,

all of Canada.

◆   ◆   ◆

When the dancer is inviolable
the choreographer, rapt,

discovers she is his subject:
dangerously malleable,

opaque as the future.
As if her neck, bending,

her spun body, nearly toppling,
were milliseconds ahead of him

beckoning.

◆   ◆   ◆

The blues recordings he learned from
were laced with scratches,

the singers aged and toothless.
To match them, he muffled his diction

taking a mouthful of potatoes
before he started his song,

wearing the words down:
the whiskered notes labor

beyond him.

La Belle Dame sans Merci

The sedge withering, yes, and that peculiar stillness,
as before a storm, when the warblers

hunker down: well, there he spoke true
(and also that part about the "sweet moan"),

but he's loitering on the cold hill's side
for his own reasons:

that in the summer I razored a long mane
into a tousle. That I never could stand

to ride sidesaddle, would rather
run on these light feet, ha, these

bare, speedy little appendages,
in the path of his "pacing steed." (He said

the horse would spook. It didn't.)
That I said I could cook

but ruined the venison. We did have honey wild.
We did have manna . . .

I wasn't the faery he wanted,
in fact, wasn't

a faery. There was another true part,
when I wept.

Ah! woe betide!
But that came later.

Mediterranean Cooking for Two

Octopus in one hand, cookbook in the other, he nearly
loses his focus over the black print, the famous chef's direction
to dash the small body against the sink's steel—"vigorously,"
according to the recipe, in imitation of Greek women
tenderizing the new catch right on the shore's wet rocks.
Here in his kitchen the sound of that flesh landing again and
       again,
flaccid and unmusical, troubles him. "Fifteen or six-
teen times," read the instructions! But something of his own
body sings in that dull sound, mortal and precarious. He
would serve the dish later that afternoon with a fine sherry,
the house already redolent of garlic and olives. *Nine. Ten.*
It *is* love: the small creature pitched and retrieved again
from the stainless cold (*thirteen*), sliced, sautéed, and oil-
drizzled: *Fifteen.* It must be. *Sixteen.* All he can handle . . .

Little Elegy for Flute

Everyone looks at the pregnant woman.
Whether she's moving or just standing there.
Let's say it's Sunday.
She's assessed, scrutinized, judged, weighed, et cetera.
Well, what do they expect?
1932.
There with her husband.
Let's take a little walk, et cetera.
Get her her fresh air.
She's just standing there when the producer.
Next to the Packard dealership.
Everyone looks.
In a huge dress, huge.
Twin-six sport phaeton in the window.
Impossible.
Or producer's assistant.
It's 1932.
For movie stars!
He asks her husband.
He says, "two weeks."
She's just standing there.
Huge.
The studio will pay, he says.
Get her some fresh air.
What?
Say yes.
For the cesarean . . .
Let's take a little walk.
The child to be lifted into the arms of an actress.
It's Sunday.
Los Angeles.
Acting adoring.

Adorable.
The "It" girl, Clara Bow, at twenty-seven.
What?
For her movie.
Say yes!

❖   ❖   ❖

It's Linda Marie's story: how her father was born. I'm remembering
it today, having wanted children for many years, then thinking the
feeling gone for some time, then having it return surreptitiously to
its old place. There was one child that almost made it. A friend has
just gone through in vitro and given birth; another friend has
become a father; new acquaintances have had their second child,
all within a month. In years past, you had children or you didn't.
Choice rarely entered in. If you yearned for a child until you could
no longer take food or drink with your husband, until your hair
grew wild and curled of its own will, until spots of blood appeared
over your heart, it changed nothing.

❖   ❖   ❖

. . . Nasa Springer (Clara Bow) is delivered of a premature baby,
after which she moves to a cheap boarding house. The baby needs
medicine. Nasa has no money: she finds a girl to sit with the child,
and sets out for the streets to pick up a man. Returning with the
prescription, she learns that a fire has broken out, and the baby
has died of smoke inhalation . . .

—from the synopsis, Call Her Savage, 1932

❖   ❖   ❖

She tells me, He's never seen that movie.
Where he was born.
Less trauma, cesarean birth.
For the baby.
It's her father, that baby.
Family story.

It was the Depression.
1932.
She assesses, scrutinizes, weighs.
In the movie, she thinks, the baby was a girl.
The baby is not so wrinkled, born this way.
The family actually didn't approve of movies.
So he never saw.
In the movie, the baby dies in the fire, I tell her.
Oh no!
Really?
She's thinking: *born then dies.*
My father?

♦   ♦   ♦

It was Clara Bow's second-to-last movie; she played a wild woman.
Uncontrollable, headstrong. Irresistible. *Call Her Savage* was one of
her three favorite films. There was *It.* There was *Mantrap.* There
was this. A year later, she fell out of favor: a bad Brooklyn voice,
they said, and too many naughty roles. How could she be a serious
actress? She left the movies then, and had her children.

♦   ♦   ♦

All that season, Farrell was dancing *Chaconne,* and at her most
luminous. I wanted every performance—*go,* he said. *Indulge
yourself.* Later I discovered that was the summer he learned his
new life: picking men up, using them quickly, cabbing fast back to
our place. And I, anon, coming in flushed from the walk uptown,
oblivious. Well, you know the ballet: it's Orpheus and Eurydice.
The adagio is a chestnut but contains that moment just before you
find out you will not actually live in this world. The flute manages
to tell you that much.

Cold Song

Kept going once I jumped from it
where you slowed for the light
or where he slowed and I can't remember now
which of you it was

I was pretty torn up but I got fixed
that's how I remember it

and turn to you in the night
your hair, your ear should be
right there

Didn't I touch gently enough?
That's why you went.

An inevitable condition of technology
is breakdown. Things don't work
like they should for me

like, I used to be able to dance?
When I see your face
from the one time I saw it
it ripples a little,
there's a sheet of rain in front,

so sometimes you look
like another person I knew,
a bad guy, it's just
the way he was.

Here it goes
snowing again:
nothing will get through on the road,

the balsams droop their branches
absurdly. A deer's standing there
laughing—

Lake Superior, Summer

I.

All season the lake
wore different dresses:
a thick gray one like
a supplicant's, or a frothy
light green one to dance in.

I approached her
from around a curve.

She could make herself
almost coy, then reveal
her new aspect:
a navy blue gown.

After the storm
she withdrew in clouded
and bruise-colored silks,
unusually placid. Like a girl
walking into a field,
leaving the lit house.

Every morning I ran by,
rounding the turn where I glimpsed her
again: first through leaves,
then fully exposed
to the sky, the ore boats, bees,
shrill gulls, that summer
music. If she spoke,
would I respond?

I wondered. Every morning,
going there. Coming back.

II.

The lid of a cooler, flung from a truck.
A curl of brown bark, ripped from a logger's cargo.
Somebody's wedding photos, tucked into a paper folder
labeled MOM. An unused roll of black electrical tape,
flung from a truck. Somebody's sunglasses, scratched,
scratched beyond usefulness (from bouncing?).
A hairband. A woman's comb. One
white athletic sock, laundered but unworn.
A chunk of split firewood, flung from a truck.
Many beer cans, one of them set tenderly upright
at the shoulder's verge: more taste! less filling!
And the green glass, the brown glass, shattered . . .
Lanyards. A gas cap, settled among the asters.
The dog in the back of a red pickup barking, his song
chasing him along the wide curve of the highway.

(III.

One by one, the photos
give up the shine-browed bride
and her sweating groom,
the reception line, the people
clutching their printed napkins
at the reception, which reveal
the date (June 29),
no names, there's no sense
that Mom would drop
these snapshots
out of her speeding car
on the way to Duluth
skirting the lake's north shore.
That's the ugliest cake
I've ever seen. You saved
the life of these pictures: now
they'll stay with you
for good. Won't they.)

IV.

For every drunk
who drives toward you on the shoulder,
thinking it's funny, there's a heron
stock-still in the ditchwater, watching you;
there's a dog glad of the company
in the two-mile stretch of his territory, panting,
his tongue like a squire's pennant.
Exchange. For every exhaust-spewing semi
whose wind-wake blasts you, there's
a sudden field of clover, waving
fragrant alongside; there's the cry
of a pileated woodpecker
you'd never have heard, and these
are precious things. Of the distances
disappearing under your footfalls:
say nothing. Run. Deny. Embrace—

Month After Month

I make my dog happy when he is sick
by taking him for a drive. In the fields outside of town, haystacks

lie rolled and left randomly by the baler—
but my dog is myopic; to him they are cows at pasture,

and he barks and barks, white paws
on the dashboard. We fly past. He's always hated cows—

big, lethargic creatures, and him so small—
he's wagging now, in control.

"What kind of person," my mother asks,
"drives her dog around with her in a car like that?" It's

her way of mourning my unproductive body.
Another month passes. Its white sky.

Depressive Episode

It's funny, but I don't remember much.
By day a rhombus travels over walls
reputed to be white: when evening falls
the lot's halogen streetlight makes the switch
and keeps the pattern of that window etched
just opposite my bed. I want to sleep.
They give me drugs that promise some escape
but fail. I have a buzzing they can't touch.
I have a clarity that I can't reach.
Words will not come. The nurses will not talk
or care for me. The doctor tells me, later,
that this, regrettably, is normal. Such
is their perspective: Someone with the luck
of health has tried to take her life. They hate her.

Later, at Mickey's

Healing is a job that requires a mop.
                    —Fanny Howe

The first symptom: emotions do not fit their cause.
The second: loss of desire to eat.
(And she who took such pleasure!)

"The government prefers to pull that tooth, not fill it,"
and so on for each of them—

then dentures so painful she didn't wear them much
and someone finally stole them while she slept.
Say what you wish: clouds won't answer.

Third: waking sharply at three in the morning
unable to sleep again.

Shirley will be at Mickey's: a short walk from the shelter.
Eating without teeth. You could go there,
sit on the next stool and nurse your coffee.
Talk meds with Shirley: what works, what's junk.
Winter nights, Mickey's is packed.

Next to the fountain, a turbaned *punkawallah*
wafts his palm fan for her. It's a grand hotel:
don't ask what goes on here.
It's open all night!

The symptoms spiral downward after this.

Today's the first real blizzard. At Mickey's,
each customer ushers the ice indoors.

Avoid high windows. Hide the knives.
Guns: no. Don't travel by train.
Don't travel. Try not to be alone.

When the guys come in with their Thermos bottles
it means dawn. Whatever you have to do,
do it now.

A Shrine

Eric Stokes. Day of the Dead, Nov. 2, 1999.

Birdcalls from a Oaxacan zocalo
and the noise of one broom.

A little fellow wearing a red mask.
Bottle of Jack.

An echo of flute.

Inland, we still smell sea in the morning,
taste salt in our mouths;

a smooth heavy stone
rolls along the floor with a low sound
toward a pair of hands.

Birdcalls from the wooded edge of a lake.

If we wept, it was not for hearing the tune,
but for the remembered words.

A grocery sack of vegetables. Bottle of wine.

The windows in this place, forever open,
allow in the cool air.

White cap. Ashes.
A pair of hands.

Kumquats

Roadfood fresh from the mesh bag,
the sunwarmed fruitstand, Florida hot.
You never drove the old Highway One
to Touristville, where the folks retired,
windows down and the hot salt air
razoring through the car,
a bag of kumquats wedged
between you
and your nubile passenger,
summer vacation, your first lover,
your first visit home, and maybe (you think)
it's for real (you
don't know any better, know
anything yet); you think marriage, yes,
it's a long drive forever on Highway One,
beach towns flapping past like flags,
like frigate birds—
                                    if you had,
you'd remember groping the bag
for its burning fruit, finding
a thumbling, warm and plump,
and running your teeth and tongue
against its dimples. Bitten,
its sour fountain and sweet,
resistant, mitigating rind
are the texture of a certain kind
of appetite. I can taste it now.
I can feel my hair
whipping back
frizzy and thick in the humid heat,
the sweat on my forehead drying
at the window. I want
you, too, to taste the kumquat

handed you by your lover:
it's ninety, you're going
eighty, it's three in the afternoon
and you are feeding each other
fruit in the front seat.
Go ahead and laugh
at its comic percussive name,
its k-kick against your soft palate,
its dumb uhs and ahs: it's not
the name you'd give it
when you taste that acid juice
and chew its pulp and realize
you've eaten the thing
whole: outside,
inside, all.

Birding

Some pursue quantity, a lifelist
personalized to the range and predilections
of a patient soul with binoculars angled up,
pencil ready, the mind's handy abacus
poised to click the next accumulation;
some seek particular birds
that return each year, old regulars
sentimental about their habits;
some just want the exotic,
the deep hues, rich excesses of rainbow
animate and winged and seldom seen.
But wild isn't always where you want it—
off the deck where the siskins fed all winter
framed by the kitchen's glass. You go
upwind of the heap of roadkill
at the highway department's utilitarian lot
where carcasses rot behind the dinosaur plows,
the graders out of season. New habitat.
What's struck by a truck goes back
to its role as provender, as surely
as if wolves patrolled these parts again:
whitetail gone to ribcage, their unaesthetic bones
marking the carnage where flyhatch
happens. Because of the semi
speeding down 61, you scope
warblers spangling the decomposing mound
with their brilliant golds,
the crimsons you covet.

Theremin

Of course, surprise.
Coming near, a sudden
woman's cry, pitch
and woo of the bodiless—

until he backs away.
He comes near: a woman's cry.

Music for the small hours
of winter mornings:

someone has disappeared
leaving behind
part voice, part chill.

Later, he thinks:
the sound of whales?
the world ending, or
ended: was this
the warning?

She holds nothing, says
nothing, picks at the air
above the box,

a madwoman.
Fixes her eyes ahead.

No veil
shadowing her,
nothing in front.

A woman stands
waving her arms.

She does not make,
or does, the otherworldly
crying—

call of an extinct
bird?

You can almost make out,
fear making out,
words

meant for you.

Lauds

One floor below, the fridge
stutters awake, makes its mechanical adjustment
the way I'd clear my throat; and from bed
I know it's late, late and dark.
There's no traffic yet on Lexington,
no low thrum of trucks idling
making deliveries on Grand, grinding trash.

But something's disturbed the dog,
who shakes herself briskly
and circles again on her pillow.
Her tags and collar tinkle high-pitched and gentle
and would not rouse me if I weren't
already wakeful, lying with my eyes
deceptively closed, as if my father
were back again. Checking on me.
Expecting me asleep.
Home from the paper past midnight,

he stood at my door letting the quarters
and thin dimes in his pocket
shift through his fingers, jingling,
his presence and the early hour
mildly announced. And though I'd watched
and waited, I hid myself
unbreathing in my child body
to keep him there, to savor
that fragile music.

Humanophone

I. George Ives

The microtones were eternal
but they'd always been *error,* a rube tenor

raucously flat in the camp meeting,
proud, while somebody snickered; a child

at his violin or slide cornet
offending the master and earning

contempt and a rapped hand.
How easy to be orthodox: harder,

to hear, with his absolute pitch,
sounds *new* rather than wrong—

his son remembered him running
drenched to the piano

from a summer storm, from churchbells
rung rain-soaked and off-key next door,

searching to match that sound and running
out again, to listen, having failed;

and later, filling the household's crystal
variously, striking the tones

that fell *between* piano keys, "sounds
as beautiful sometimes as they were funny—

a complex that only children
are old enough to appreciate,"

building ever-more-fantastic
contraptions to capture them: sounds

unjudged, gathered in, orphans
embraced for the first time—

II.

the *humanophone*—an instrument made up of singers,
each of whom sang a single tone, and only
when called upon by the music;

a machine of twenty-four violin strings stretched
over a laundry-press, and tuned to whatever microtones
he fancied (suppressed by his family,
who could not abide the chords the invention made);

a piano tuned to match the sounds
of overtones;

a band placed on a roof, to play variations
of what the band in the village green was playing;

new scales free of octaves;

unsuccessful attempts, using Danbury Pond,
to make the sound of an echo—its tonal color,
diminished volume; its quality a subtle twin
to the original tone—

III.

After getting used to hearing a piano piece
when the upper melody, runs, etc.,
were filled out with quarter-tone notes
(as a kind of ornamentation),
when the piece was played on the piano alone
there was a very keen sense of dissatisfaction—
of something wanted
but missing—

IV. Song for a Five-Note Humanophone

                A-   merican
                               vision:
to dis-   pose
of re-   ceived
                          i-   deas,
      or ac-   cept
                        them   only
                        as   points
                        from   which to
                        let
             go:
                        that
was   nineteenth-
             century
                                 hyp-   o-
             crisy.   How quickly
             they
             closed
                        in
             on the   second-
                        story
             poet, the   genius
                        bandleader's
                        genius
             son—

V.

—like the excruciating absence
of Virgil in Paradise, when Dante turns
after all their journey
to share a thought with him:
                              nothing now—
his old guide gone—

Charles Ives has one last message from his father
        (*Tell Parker that every dissonance*
        doesn't have to resolve
        if it doesn't happen to feel like it, any more
        than every horse
        should have its tail bobbed
        just because it's the
        prevailing fashion)
who is, three weeks later, dead—
heart attack, silence—

the democracy of sounds
now foundering. Where
can the boy take his songs,
if not past the place his father
brought him to? Over the high mountain,
without a guide—

VI. Song for a Three-Note Humanophone

Don't

pay   *too*

           much

    attention

to the   *sounds.*

If you   *do,*

you   *may*

    miss

the   *mu-*

sic.

You   *won't*

get a   *heroic*

    ride to   *hea-*

ven on   *pretty*

    little

    sounds—

Partch Stations

Harry Partch, 1901–1974

I. He Appeareth Before the Audience, Is Condemned

You only put that music on to annoy people, she said.
—I've forgotten who. Friend of a friend, some party,

but a thrill roils from it: when Partch sets Li Po

> *I heard someone in the Yellow Crane House*
> *playing on the sweet bamboo flute*
> *the tune of falling plum flowers*

he doesn't score a flute's song, but a man
reaching to describe his memory of it
with a vocal imitation,
            his *who-hoo-oo-oos* in a high voice,
higher than he would usually use;

a man telling a story about something
he *heard*
            and wants you to hear, too . . .

> *Much of that which is man-made we ignore, such as*
> *the music of speech. Well, I'm not ignoring it.*

The plucked viola like a long-legged insect
picks its way around the fallen petals.

Nobody likes this, she said.

II. He Faileth to Be Born in China

Forgive him in his wishes and delusions: he is beset.

Chinese lullabies (the only ones she knew) from his missionary mother;

Mandarin from his gone-atheist father, faithlost in Shantung Province;

furniture of black bamboo, Sung Dynasty paintings they'd bought there;

> *more books in Chinese, accordion-folded, with ivory thongs, illustrated*
> *by gory colored lithographs of the beheading of missionaries, than books in*
> *English;*

these he remembers from childhood:

they so stamp their impress that he claims he, too, sparked to life

in China—conceived in a Boxer prison camp—or later, at sea,

learning in the womb for all time his mother's queasiness as they fled—

but no:

   alone of his siblings he is Californian, all.

He would have accepted that from his parents: birth in China.

(Perhaps *only* that.)

            It would have explained many things—

OCCUPANT IS A HEATHEN CHINEE, the note on his last door sang.

III. He Consigneth His Music to the Fire

. . . in pursuing the respectable, the widely accepted,
I had not been faithful.

He has been unfaithful,
and thus does he purify himself:
    the piano concerto
    the string quartet
    the symphonic poem
    the popular songs
    everything he has written

hideously unsuited to my needs

ash in the depths of a pot-bellied stove.

Take that, self.

    And here too the sinning arm, which wrote it: burn.
    And both transgressive ears.
    Ambitious heart—
    All burn.

        As late as 1960 I was still pulling out bits of ideas
        from that pot-bellied stove, ideas stored away
        in memory—
                that mysterious structure of cells and spirit—

Everything must be proven in the fire.

    Here spark a few live cells—

What is tempered? What dies?

IV. He Heareth the Voice

I see little evidence that poets have studied
the sounds of their own voices...

He liked to cite the Emperor Chun (from 2300 B.C.):
Let the music follow the sense of the words.

The unborn listen for months
to their mothers, and, born,
they turn for that one song
conducted through bone,
through fluid and dark:

it's different now—harsher—
and the world all glare—

      and some search years
      for that wordmusic,
      the mother's filtered tone
      speaking inward, to *one*—

Harry insists *all* speech
holds melody and rhythm:
not hers alone.

      I needed other scales and other instruments.

Li Po speaks unaffectedly;
and Hobo Pablo in his letter, the newsboys
crying through the fog of San Francisco:

he heareth the many voices, that we may hear.

V. He Stretcheth a Viola by the Neck

Partch is peevish.
There isn't room on this fingerboard
to find all the notes.

Should be 43 in each octave:
they all mush together.

(People are already laughing somewhere.
    Forgive them—)

Edward Bentin helps him:
fixes a cello fingerboard to the viola
and Harry marks the stops with fractions and brads,

cradles the soundbox between his knees
gingerly, to calm it.

Two over one: the diapason,
the octave. Greek first, then the Latin.
Three over two. The diapente.
Sesquialterate.
In just intonation, a "perfect fifth." And so on.

Translation:

First he hears the Beloved speaking low.

The song comes.

To write the song down
he must invent notation.
To play it, he must become
a carpenter, building new instruments
that respond to the melodies he hears.

To perform the song
he must teach all the musicians
and all the singers who will ever present it
the notations, the instruments—

You see where this is leading.
You have been there.

He is a long time alone—

VI. He Dreameth the Kithara

Old woman copied the kithara from a Greek vase in the British Museum he wanted it.

She found someone to build it for her during the war, there was no wood, the guy used an orange box somebody threw out it got a good tone.

She let him examine.

Partch was thinking, *I could get an orange box.*

She figured out the tuning, being an expert on *auloi* and Greek *harmoniai,* but he wanted his own tuning and more strings arranged in chords and wanted it bigger.

I must have one. Also the design could be improved.

Plectra on every finger—

He awakens in Anderson Creek with a redwood timber from the wrecked bridge, thinking *a base for the kithara—*

Thinking *that dream was so real I could smell taste touch it.*

VII. He Wandereth as a Hobo

Getting a ride in California: could take days,
counting the gone cars slash by slash in pencil
with a rail through for the fifth

like this railing preventing the cars from diving
down from the asphalt, wrecking, their drivers thrown
and dead, the bum still stranded

in Barstow, California, still without prospects.
February 1940: cold, waiting.
He fingers the smooth rail: reads

two months' worth of hobo graffiti inscribed there—
where handouts are good, where someone is headed
if only a ride would stop;

or who wants a husband or a wife—*eloquent
in what it fails to express in words.* Music
hides in this everyday speech:

Harry is homeless when he hears its lost singing,
one voice, the tradition of China, of Greece,
India, Arabia,

the words matter, guiding the music; the singer
accompanies himself on an instrument
like an ancient Celtic bard.

He rideth the rails all through the Great Depression;
he dishwasheth, picketh California fields,
readeth proof for newspapers—

a week, a month at a time. In the Wilderness
he hones his theories, he dreams his new works
unhindered. And moves along.

VIII. He Buildeth the Chromelodeon

A six-2/1 harmonium from which the old reeds were removed and into which reeds of the forty-three-degree Monophonic scale were placed, in sequence, so that the new 2/1 covers a much wider keyboard extent—three and a half octaves.

All along he had heard it in his head,
never aloud.

Now *you* can hear it.

Your hand can't make an octave on these
multicolored keys

(not that *octave* means anything anymore—).

All the surfaces in his room covered, you notice,
with pill bottles.

He's on a weird diet, too: he mentioned it.

Bowles, attending an early performance, wrote
The audience

convulsed, asked for it again, whereupon the piece,

*which had given one the impression of being
an inspired*

improvisation by a group of maniacs, impossible to reperform,

*was repeated
as exactly as if it had been a playback.*

At the verge of the room, with its striped keys numbered,

it beckons you. *Go ahead and try it,*
he says.

IX. He Wandereth with His Instruments

Wisconsin	Two tons of instruments on his back,
to El Centro	the hobo in him can't settle
to Gualala	just anywhere:
to Oakland	needs
to Mills College	space
to Sausalito	and isolation
to Urbana	for rehearsing musicians,
to Yellow Springs	proper storage conditions, cheap rent.
to Chicago	Fifty-
to Northwestern University	five times he
to Urbana	relocates his private and fragile
to CoEd	orchestra. Fifteen times in sixteen years,
to Springfield	he counts up on a scrap of paper (why?).
to Petaluma	As a hobo, he carried a viola case:
to Del Mar	for viola and
to L.A.	clothes—

X. He Playeth the Marimba Eroica

The instrument requires a player with robust shoulders, back, arms.
If he possesses this equipment, and is also something of a percussionist,
the playing of the instrument is not difficult . . .

It is his visual *aspect that the Eroica player must cultivate.*
He must give the impression of a sure winner.
In exciting and furious passages
he must look like Ben Hur in his chariot,
charging around the last curve of the final lap.

XI. He Hangeth the Cloud-Chamber Bowls

Or, he taketh a turn toward percussion.

As in, he maketh many marimbas

from bamboo, pernambuco wood, hormigo,
padouk, rosewood, redwood, and Sitka spruce.
Sands them to tune them.

He has already rejected electronic possibilities.

Prefers his harmonium to an electric pump organ
for its deferent response to the performer.

We observe here his moment of crossing-over:

a temptation of Pyrex carboys
from the Berkeley Radiation Lab.

Let him among you who could resist, etc.

Besides, they were a gift.

Sawed in half they made the most
delicious gongs
                    (deep bells).

When he stands behind them, playing,

their curved transparencies surround him
like so many noisy haloes . . .

XII. He Vieweth the Gourd Tree

The future needs the sensuality and corporeality in music of the same kind that Walt Whitman gave to poetry.

Literally in a trashpile.
A eucalyptus branch
scavenged, dragged home dead:

he made a base for it, made
a tree of it, with fruit
of Chinese temple bells

hanging ripe—*like papayas,*
he thought, *the smallest
at the top . . .* It looked

almost alive, colt-awkward,
gangly. Oddly passive.
Conceived

*in dynamic relationship
with a human body—*
who glides around it

and strikes.
Dance and song
and an instrument

accompanying:
an Ancient, come back,
would recognize.

XIII. He Speaketh to the Audience

The creative artist acquires a shade of anarchism

that after several decades of weathering, begins to bear
the strange patina of the recidivist, the unregenerate criminal.

We as a people give loving attention to details of individual crime
from a perfectly logical envy of the criminal: crime is one area

where individuality is taken for granted.
This is hardly the case in the creative arts.

I am a profound traditionalist, but of an unusual sort.

We are trapped by our own machines,
which tend, progressively, to remove us from nature.

My instruments are absolutely primitive.
They are visual, as are those at a Congo ritual.

The players move in a way to excite the eye.
This is not an abstract communication

but something that will agitate our Cro-Magnon genes.

XIV. He Wandereth After His Death

Tell me Ulysses, you say you've traveled around the world, have you ever been arrested?

Nobody likes this music, somebody says—
but the audience
has wandered away from her

◆　◆　◆

His vagrancy gone chronic,
the ashes tumble piecemeal to the Pacific.

Here at the last station you can barely
make out his white hair.

The instruments, without him, travel
familiar patterns of eviction: they circle.

◆　◆　◆

Let not one year pass—I now say to myself—when I do not step one significant century, or millennium, backward.

◆　◆　◆

There are rides on the highway at Green River, but they go right on by. There are rides on the freights at Green River, too, but the Green River bull says:

"You exclamation mark bum! Get your semicolon asterisk out o' these yards, and don't let me catch you down here again, or you'll get thirty days in the jailhouse!"

◆　◆　◆

In Petaluma, the tune of falling roses
and camellias

echoes eighth-century China, vibrating
the steel strings.

◆　◆　◆

*I hold no wish for the obsolescence of our present widely heard
instruments and music.*

I feel that more ferment is necessary to a healthy musical culture.

I am endeavoring to instill more ferment.

Notes

"Saintmaker": For Luisito Lujan.

"Celebration on the Planet Mars":

Raymond Scott (born Harry Warnow), 1908–94, was a jazz composer and bandleader whose work is best known as background music for Warner Brothers cartoons. He was also an inventor of electronic instruments, working mostly in solitude, but occasionally with the help of a Columbia University student he met in 1957, Robert Moog. Efforts are now being made to preserve the decades of recordings he left behind and his one remaining intact invention, the Electronium. Titles in quotation marks are titles of Raymond Scott compositions.

Scott's six-piece ensemble, which performed between 1937 and 1939 (and was revived with different musicians in 1948–49), was called the Raymond Scott Quintette. (He liked the sound of the word better than "sextet.") The *down beat* anecdote is retold in Irwin Chusid's notes to the CD *Celebration on the Planet Mars: A Tribute to Raymond Scott* (Koch 3-7909-2). Shirley Temple's movie *Rebecca of Sunnybrook Farm* made use of Scott's composition "The Toy Trumpet," to which Temple and Bill "Bojangles" Robinson danced a tap duet. Scott's "Powerhouse" was used 43 times in Warner Brothers cartoons; his compositions were used 133 times in 117 Warner Brothers cartoons overall. The first sentence in Section V is Scott's, quoted with slight modification from Irwin Chusid ("Raymond Scott's Push-Button Musical Universe," *Mix*, October 1993).

"Reading Dante": For Charles Bell.

"Mediterranean Cooking for Two": For David Nolf.

"Little Elegy for Flute": For Linda Marie Zaerr.

"A Shrine": For Eric Stokes.

"Kumquats": For G. E. Patterson.

"Birding": For Vern Gersh and Terry McLaughlin.

"Humanophone":

George Ives, father of Charles Ives, was a Civil War regimental band-leader at the age of nineteen and more an innovative thinker about music than an actual composer. He was his son's first and most important teacher, grounding him not only in academic musical theory and technique, but also imparting his own unconventional ideas about tones and sounds. Sources for the poem include *Charles Ives and His Music*, by Henry Cowell and Sidney Cowell (Oxford: Oxford University Press, 1955), and David Wooldridge, *From the Steeples and Mountains* (New York: Knopf, 1974). The quotations in sections I, III, and VI are from a 1925 article Charles Ives wrote for *Pro Musica Quarterly*, which was in turn quoted in Cowell and Cowell. Section VI is a quotation from George Ives. Section II's information about George Ives's inventions and experiments is also from Cowell and Cowell.

Sections IV and VI: Each tabulation represents a different pitch; the tones rise from left to right.

Section V: *Purgatorio* XXX. Charles Ives, born in 1874 in Danbury, Connecticut, was to be as misread and misunderstood by his mentor, Horatio Parker, at Yale, as Emily Dickinson was by her literary friend, Colonel Thomas Wentworth Higginson. Parker continually ignored or "corrected" Ives's innovations.

"Partch Stations":

Harry Partch (1901–74) was a composer whose works were based on just intonation and were largely performed upon instruments he invented to accommodate that system. He spent eight years during the Depression living as a hobo, and drew upon hobo writings and lore for much of his early work. Sources for the poem include *Genesis of a Music*, by Harry Partch (Madison: University of Wisconsin Press, 1949); *Bitter Music*, by Harry Partch, edited by Thomas McGeary (Urbana: University of Illinois Press); *Enclosure 3*, edited by Philip Blackburn (St. Paul, Minn.: American Composers Forum, 1997); and *Harry Partch: A Biography*, by Bob Gilmore (New Haven: Yale University Press, 1998).

I: Li Po quotation from *Seventeen Lyrics by Li Po*, Harry Partch.
II: quoted from Gilmore. Note on door reproduced in Blackburn.
III: epigraph and quotations from Gilmore.
IV: epigraph from Blackburn (from a Partch letter to David Bowen, October 3, 1960). Other quotes in Partch, *Genesis of a Music*.
VII: quotation from Partch's article "Barstow," printed in the *Carmel Pine Cone*, September 16, 1941, reprinted in Blackburn.
VIII: Chromelodeon description from Partch, *Genesis of a Music*. Long excerpt from Paul Bowles, *New York Herald-Tribune*, April 23, 1944, quoted in Blackburn.

IX: list culled from Partch's notations, 1964, reproduced in Black-
       burn.

X: quoted directly from "Manual on the Maintenance and Repair
       of—and the Musical and Attitudinal Techniques for—Some Puta-
       tive Musical Instruments," 1963, reproduced in Blackburn.

XII: epigraph: Partch, quoted in *Women's Wear Daily,* January 17, 1967.
       "Papayas" quotation adapted from Gilmore; "dynamic relation-
       ship" passage adapted from Partch quotation in *Art in America,*
       no. 6, December 1964, excerpted in Blackburn.

XIII: adapted from Partch's address at Columbia University, April 9,
       1952.

XIV: epigraph: quoted from *Ulysses Turns Back from the Edge of the World,*
       in "Three Cups of Wine with Partch," by Les Scher, U.C.L.A. *Daily
       Bruin,* May 4, 1966, reproduced in Blackburn. "Let not one year
       pass . . ." from "Fragments from Partch, for BMI file, 1968," repro-
       duced in Blackburn. "There are rides . . ." quoted from *U.S. High-
       ball,* included in *Bitter Music.* "I hold no wish . . ." excerpts from
       "Plans for Work," Guggenheim application, September 11, 1942.

Janet Holmes

is author of *The Green Tuxedo*, which received the Ernest Sandeen Prize in Poetry from the University of Notre Dame, and *The Physicist at the Mall*, which Joy Harjo selected for the Anhinga Prize in 1994. *The Green Tuxedo* was named the *ForeWord* Magazine Book of the Year in Poetry, and was awarded the 1999 Minnesota Book Award.

Holmes's poems were chosen by W. S. Merwin for the Pablo Neruda Prize in 1997 and received the Chad Walsh Prize from *Beloit Poetry Journal* in 1999. They have twice been selected to appear in editions of *The Best American Poetry,* and have been published in *American Poetry Review, Antaeus, Boulevard, The Georgia Review, Poetry, Prairie Schooner,* and many other journals. Holmes teaches in the M.F.A. in Creative Writing program at Boise State University and directs Ahsahta Press.